Arena-Taschenbuch

Band 2425

KNISTER,
geboren 1952, lebt in Wesel.
KNISTER schreibt Bücher,
macht Musikkassetten und CD-ROMs.
Verrückt, lustig und spannend. Immer!
Lieblingsfarbe: BUNT.
Lieblingsessen: Spagetti zu jeder Tageszeit.
Hobby: In einer Rockband spielen.
Sternzeichen: Frosch.

Ellen Butzko,
geboren 1963, ist Englischlehrerin an einem Gymnasium,
als Fachleiterin auch in der Referendarausbildung
tätig und Mitglied einer Arbeitsgruppe zur
Grundschuldidaktik.

Birgit Rieger
ist im Harz aufgewachsen, wo sich bekanntermaßen die Hexen scharenweise tummeln. Kein Wunder dass sie Lilli gleich in ihr Herz geschlossen hat, als sie 1992 zum ersten Mal von ihr las. Inzwischen haben Birgits Hexe-Lilli-Zeichnungen die Kinder auf der ganzen Welt verzaubert. Außer ihrem Beruf liebt die Kinderbuchillustratorin ihren frechen roten Tigerkater und das Verreisen (wie Lilli!).
Sie lebt mit ihrem Mann in Berlin.

KNISTER

Lilli the Witch at Vampire Castle

Englische Textfassung von
Ellen Butzko

Mit Illustrationen von
Birgit Rieger

MIX
Papier aus verantwortungsvollen Quellen
FSC® C110508
www.fsc.org

5. Auflage als Arena-Taschenbuch 2015

Englische Fassung von *Hexe Lilli auf Schloss Dracula*

Englische Fassung: Ellen Butzko

Umschlaggestaltung und Innenillustrationen: Birgit Rieger
Gesamtherstellung: Westermann Druck Zwickau GmbH
ISSN 0518-4002
ISBN 978-3-401-02425-7

www.arena-verlag.de

Vampire words

vampire – Vampir
turn into a vampire – zum Vampir werden
vampire slayer – Vampirjäger
defend oneself against – sich wehren gegen
suck blood – Blut saugen
garlic – Knoblauch
glove – Handschuh
turn to dust – zu Staub werden
wooden stake – Holzpflock
coffin – Sarg
dusk – Dämmerung
scream – schreien
bat – Fledermaus
cellar – Keller
alive – lebend, am Leben
full moon – Vollmond
midnight – Mitternacht
book of witchcraft – Hexenbuch
trick of witchcraft – Zaubertrick

Lilli the Witch at Vampire Castle

This is Lilli.
She's your age
and looks like
a normal child.
She *is* a normal
child, but . . .
not really. Lilli has a book.
This is *not* a normal book:
it's a book of witchcraft.
One morning Lilli looks under her bed –
and surprise, surprise:
there it is, the book of witchcraft!
Lilli has no idea who put it there.
But she knows that
the book is full of real magic
and wild tricks of witchcraft.
Lilli can do some of these tricks.
But be careful!

If *you* do these tricks,
it can be very dangerous:
one wrong word and –
a magic broom turns into a skateboard,
a teacher turns into a penguin,
ice-cream turns into a schnitzel.
That's why nobody knows
that Lilli has this book.
That's why nobody knows
that she's a secret witch.
And that's why Leon doesn't know
that she can do magic tricks.
Who's Leon?
He's Lilli's little brother.
Leon asks lots of questions.
Little brothers can really
get on your nerves!
But Lilli also loves her
little brother very much . . .

Let's begin our story then.

schnitzel – Schnitzel (das gibt es tatsächlich in Amerika so!)
can get on your nerves – kann dir auf die Nerven gehen

Chapter 1

Lilli is sitting on her bed.
She's got her little stuffed toy mouse
in her hand –
and in her mouth.
But she's so nervous
she doesn't know that she's got her
stuffed toy mouse's ear in her mouth.

stuffed toy mouse – Stoffmaus

And why is she so nervous?
Because she's reading about vampires:
that they live in Transylvania.
That they suck blood.
That they hate garlic.
That there's a way to defend
oneself against them.
That there's a way to kill them.
And that's why Lilli now wants to
go to Transylvania.
She's got the two things that are
very important for this trip:
She knows a great magic spell to
take her there – the witch's leap.
And she's got a real vampire's glove.
It belongs to Victor, the vampire kid.
The witch's leap can only work with

witch's leap – Hexensprung
can only work – kann nur funktionieren

something from the original time and place – the glove!

It will be a wild adventure.

It will be mega dangerous!

Lilli knows that she must prepare herself.

So she makes a list for her trip to Transylvania.

She writes down:

will – wird
adventure – Abenteuer
prepare herself – sich vorbereiten

Small mirror

With a small mirror you can test
who's a vampire and who's not.
If a vampire looks into the mirror,
you can't see him in it!

Garlic

Lilli must have garlic, a lot of garlic.

mirror – Spiegel

This is the best protection against vampires. So she must buy fresh garlic and make a necklace out of it.

Extremely strong flashlight

Vampires turn to dust when they see the sun.

That's why you see them only in the dark.

An extremely strong flashlight can help you to find them.

Wooden stake

If you want to kill a vampire, you must do it with a wooden stake – right through his heart.

But you can only do that in the daytime when he's in his coffin.

protection – Schutz
necklace – Halsband
flashlight – Taschenlampe

Sunglasses

When a vampire looks at you, it's sometimes very hard to take your eyes off of him. Then you can't move until it's dark. That's when they become active. Lilli doesn't know if sunglasses can help her against vampires, but it's good to come prepared.

Ear plugs

Before a vampire dies, he screams one last time.

This is so horrible that the scream is sometimes enough to give the vampire slayer a heart attack.

Lilli doesn't want to kill a vampire.

But she does want to be prepared.

move – sich bewegen
ear plugs – Wachskügelchen
horrible – grauenvoll

Binoculars

It's always better to stay far away from vampires.

With binoculars you can keep your distance.

Clothes

Lilli must have two types of clothes:

1. Vampire's teeth and white make-up: that's her vampire outfit.
2. Sunglasses and a dark cape: that's her vampire slayer outfit.

Magic spells

Lilli wants to be prepared.

So she writes down two or three magic spells that she can use against vampires.

binoculars – Fernglas
cape – Umhang
magic spells – Zaubersprüche

Lilli has a lot of work to do now. She reads more books about vampires and gets together all the things for her dangerous trip. She's got two pairs of sunglasses, old ones and new, trendy ones. "Let's take both pairs," Lilli says to herself and that's what she does.

Lilli can't wait until Saturday when she wants to start . . .

Saturday night! Leon is in bed. Her mother is in bed, too.
Lilli puts on her rucksack with everything she has prepared.
She puts her stuffed toy mouse into the pocket of her jeans. Without the mouse she can't come home again.
The witch's leap can only work with something from the original time and place!
Then she picks up the vampire's glove that will take her to Transylvania.
Yuk, that smells old!
She also puts on the garlic necklace.

yuk – igitt

Ugh, that stinks!
She sets the alarm on her watch, because she must be back early on Sunday, before her mother and Leon are up.
Now she's ready. She presses the white glove to her heart and says her magic spell.
WOW! She slowly floats out of the room . . .

slowly floats – schwebt langsam

Chapter 2

Lilli can feel the wind in her hair.

She's cold.

She can't see anything.

Then she lands.

The wind has stopped.

She opens her eyes.

She now can see a castle.

The walls are very dark.

Lilli can see faces on the walls – evil faces.

"A magic castle," Lilli thinks.

But this is strange.

The sun's shining here. She must be in a different time zone. No vampires around.

evil – böse
strange – seltsam

Lilli feels happy and a little sad at the same time.
She's happy because she's a little bit afraid of the vampires.
But she's sad because she wants to meet real vampires!
So now she has time to walk around

the castle before it gets dark. (And before the vampires come . . .)
The entrance to the castle is wide open. A trick? There are also two small doors.
“Careful, Lilli,“ she says to herself and walks in.
Then she stops.
Someone is crying somewhere. But no, now it’s very quiet again. Lilli can feel the cold air from inside the castle. It gives her goosebumps.
“Don’t worry, Lilli,“ she says to herself.
It’s not dark, so all the vampires must be in their coffins. It’s not dangerous –

entrance – Eingang
quiet – still, leise
inside – innen, outside – außen
it gives her goosebumps – sie bekommt eine Gänsehaut

well, not mega dangerous – to look at them at this time of day. If they wake up, Lilli can run outside into the sunlight. Lilli is sure that they must be in the cellar, where it's really dark. She checks if the garlic necklace is still there and takes her stuffed toy mouse out of her pocket. If things go wrong, she can say the words of the witch's leap.

She also takes the wooden stake out of her rucksack.

Then Lilli walks down the stairs.

She's too afraid to use her flashlight.

She comes to a door.

She opens it a little bit.

It makes a horrible creak.

creak – Knarren

Lilli is totally shocked.

She can't move.

She stands and waits . . . Nothing.

Then she giggles.

This is better than a scary movie!

She walks on.

She is still holding on to her stuffed toy mouse. And now she can see the whole room. WOW!

There are ten or twelve coffins in it.

One is very small.

giggles – kichert
scary movie – Gruselfilm

She opens the small coffin a little bit . . .

“Stop, Lilli,“ she says to herself. “How can I forget?“

Vampires sleep with their eyes open. If she looks at a sleeping vampire, it can be <u>deadly</u>.

The sunglasses! Lilli takes out her trendy sunglasses from her rucksack.

And now she lifts the <u>lid</u>.

deadly – tödlich
lid – Deckel

In the coffin lies Victor, the vampire kid. Good, because Lilli's not afraid of him, she knows she's got power over him. He looks funny with his one white glove. Lilli puts the other glove back inside the coffin.
"Surprise, surprise, little Victor,"
Lilli says.
Now Lilli's got the courage to look at the mega dangerous vampires.

courage – Mut

She goes to the biggest coffin. "Stop, Lilli," she says to herself. "How can I forget?" She must be better prepared for the mega dangerous vampire.
First she puts the ear plugs into her ears. You never know . . . Then she takes the second pair of sunglasses out of her rucksack and puts them over the trendy ones.
She wants to lift the lid of the coffin. But she needs both hands because it's so heavy. She puts her stuffed toy mouse between her teeth.
BANG! BANG! The heavy lid suddenly falls to the ground.

heavy – schwer
between her teeth – zwischen die Zähne

Lilli looks into the scary eyes of an old vampire. He's horrible. She can't move. Her two pairs of sunglasses don't help her.

Oh no! Now the vampire moves.

Slowly, very slowly he rises from his coffin.

Lilli wants to scream. She opens her mouth, but no sound comes out.

Now the vampire lifts his hands . . . slowly . . . and Lilli still can't move . . . but then he smells something.

rises – richtet sich auf
sound – Ton

"Yuk, garlic . . ."

He turns his head and takes his eyes off Lilli for a second.

But that's enough for her.

She runs out of the cellar, up the stairs, through the door and out into the light. She loses her two pairs of sunglasses. "It doesn't matter," she says to herself.

turns (off) – dreht (weg)
loses – verliert
it doesn't matter – egal, es macht nichts

She's safe now.
The sun is still shining.
But it will be dark soon.
Lilli wants to be home before it's dark.
Two bats land behind her,
but she can't hear them with her ear plugs in . . .

Chapter 3

Lilli's sitting outside the castle.
"How strange, it's so quiet," she says to herself. "Ah, I've still got the ear plugs in my ears."
She takes them out and hears something behind her.
She turns around – two bats. "Oh no!"
She's shocked.
She can only think: they're vampires in the shape of bats.
But the sun is deadly for vampires.
That's what her vampire books say.
Are the books wrong?
"You must be from Honeybrook," one of the bats says.
"Honeybrook?" Lilli doesn't get it.
And the other bat says: "You're very

in the shape of bats – in Fledermausgestalt

brave! Going down into the cellar and opening Count Dracula's coffin."

"Count Dracula?" Lilli still doesn't understand.

And the first bat says: "You must be the first person to come out alive."

"Alive?" Lilli asks. "Then you're not . . ."

"Vampires? Not all bats are vampires," they say.

brave – mutig

Lilli has got an idea. She takes out her mirror and holds it in front of the two bats. Oh good, she clearly can see two bats in

the mirror. What's that now? Someone is crying somewhere. "Do you know what that is?" she asks the bats.
"Fresh blood for Count Dracula. People from Honeybrook," they say.
Lilli doesn't understand.
"Come with us," the big bat says and flies through one of the side doors.
The bats take her to a small cell.

cell – (Kerker-)Zelle

The door is locked. Four children and two adults are inside.
Lilli knows that she must help them.
She can't go home now.
She looks in her rucksack and takes out the paper with her magic spells – and after six or seven magic words the door opens and they can come out.
But they're very, very weak. "There

adults – Erwachsene
weak – geschwächt

isn't much blood inside them," Lilli thinks, "maybe they're vampires now?" She holds the mirror in front of them. She can see five of them clearly, but she can't really see the smallest girl in it.

"I must take them home quickly," Lilli says. It's dusk now. "How can I take them home?" Lilli asks the bats.

"You can use their old carriage, we can show you where it is," the bats say.

The people from Honeybrook are so

carriage – Kutsche

weak that Lilli has to help them into the carriage.
She must harness the horses – not easy, but she can do it. Good thing that Lilli's friend Mona has got a horse herself. That's how she knows what she has to do now.
And then she must steer the carriage – not easy, but she can do it.
It's late, there's not much light.
Lilli hasn't got much time. They ride down the hill from the castle.
Lilli makes the horses go faster and faster. There are no houses, no people, nothing.
Now it's completely dark.

harness the horses – die Pferde einspannen
steer – lenken
hill – Berg, Hügel

“Honeybrook,“ one of the bats says and Lilli can see a small town. There’s a wall around the town and there’s garlic everywhere on the wall. They get to the gates of the town and again there’s garlic all over the gates. Lilli can’t see any people in the town. All the streets are empty.
Lilli stops the carriage in the town square.
“Help!“ – Nobody comes.
“You must help me.“ – All quiet.
“Your people are back.“ – Not a sound.
“They’re back from the castle.“ – Nothing.
But Lilli knows that the people from

wall – Mauer
gates – (Stadt-)Tore
town square – Marktplatz

Honeybrook are watching her. She's got an idea. She talks to the two bats – and she speaks very loudly. Everybody must hear Lilli now.

"Thank you, my sweet bats. You've helped me so much.

Thank you and have some garlic."

She takes the garlic from her necklace and gives it to the two bats. But they don't want to eat the garlic.

“Please help me, please eat it,“ Lilli says quietly and then they do it. What a good trick! All the people are coming out of their houses now. They’re so happy that their friends are still alive. They want to have a big party. Somebody has come back alive from Dracula’s castle! They’re bringing medicine so their weak friends can become strong again. And they’re bringing something to eat and drink for the rest. And they all want to speak to Lilli, the vampire slayer.

They all have only one question:

“Was it horrible when you killed him?“

Lilli asks: “Killed . . .?“

Then they say: “Killed him with your wooden stake.“

Lilli answers: “They’re not dead. They’re all still alive, all of them.“

Now it’s very quiet in Honeybrook.

Nobody says a word. The people want to go back into their houses.
They're afraid.
They say: "The vampires will come and get us. You must help us. Please. Can't you defend us against the vampires?"
Lilli thinks and thinks, but she hasn't got an idea. She only asks: "When does the sun come up in the morning?"
"Between four and half past four," is the answer.
That doesn't help very much.
Lilli has got a new question:
"But how can they get inside the town? All the walls and all the gates are full of garlic."
The people answer: "We don't

understand. But they get in. And when there's a full moon, they're horrible."

Lilli looks up – tonight there's a full moon.

And then she hears the church bells. Twelve o' clock. Midnight. Vampire hour.

church bells – Kirchenglocken

Chapter 4

The church bells!
Lilli has got a great idea.
She will defend the town against the vampires.
She wants to say something but she can’t. The priest comes running.
He is screaming: “They are coming.
Bats. Lots of bats!“
The people want to run away. Lilli quickly puts her idea to them. “You must do this, please!“ But are they listening?
Lilli’s now alone. It’s very dark.
The moon is behind a big cloud.
She’s afraid. She wants to go home, to her brother Leon and her mother.

priest – Pfarrer
cloud – Wolke

But then she thinks: “No. No. No. I can do it. I can defend the town!“ She runs up the stairs of the bell tower. She takes the binoculars out of her rucksack and looks through them. She can see the bats. They land outside the town gates. There are seven of them.
And then they turn into vampires. The biggest vampire is in front. They now walk up to the gate.

Darn! Now Lilli can't see them anymore. They're behind the houses.

"Get to work, Lilli," she says to herself. This is her plan: she changes the clock.

It's not easy – but she can do it.

The hour hand is heavy. She turns it, one, two, three, four times.

It is now five minutes before four o'clock.

Then she waits for the vampires.

Her heart beats very loud.

She can see Count Dracula now.

He's in the town square.

darn! – verflixt!
changes the clock – verstellt die Uhr
hour hand – Stundenzeiger
(heart) beats – (Herz) schlägt

But something very strange is going on. Lilli looks through her binoculars. Then she giggles.
The vampires have got clothes pegs on their noses! And that's why they don't smell the garlic.
It's so simple.
But brilliant.

clothes pegs – Wäscheklammern

Lilli looks through the binoculars again.
Oh no! They've got people from Honeybrook.
Count Dracula screams: "I want the first bite!" He takes a young girl and makes to bite her in the neck.
Lilli looks at the church clock.
Only seconds before four o'clock.
Long seconds. Never ending seconds.
Then the bells toll.
ONE, TWO, THREE, FOUR.
Count Dracula looks up at the church clock:
"That can't be right! It must be a few minutes after midnight!"
And the other vampires say:

bite – Biss
toll – schlagen

"Yes, how can that be? It must be a few minutes after midnight!"
Count Dracula laughs:
"These idiots! They're trying to play a trick on us. But we're too clever for them. We can see through their foul trick."
And again he goes for the neck of the young girl.
But what's that? A rooster is crowing.
And another. And then a third rooster crows.
This is part two of Lilli's plan: the people from Honeybrook wait for the church bells and then they pinch their roosters very hard so that they crow.

A rooster is crowing. – Ein Hahn kräht.
pinch – kneifen

Now the vampires can hear the roosters from all sides.
They panic! They want to go back to their castle now. They're afraid of the sun.
But Count Dracula says again: "It's just a foul trick. Keep cool."

But he’s not very cool himself. He’s also a little bit afraid.
The vampires look up at the moon.
They can see that it’s still very dark.
They say: “Yes, it’s just a foul trick.
We’re too clever for them.“
Lilli is prepared for the next part of her plan.

“Just wait, you creeps!“
She takes the flashlight out of her rucksack and turns it on.
The strong flash of light shines directly in Count Draculas eyes.
“Oh no,“ he screams. “The first flash of sunlight! The sun is coming up. We must go home. Quickly!“

creeps – blöde Kerle
flash of light – Lichtstrahl

Seven vampires turn into seven bats and fly home.
Now they really can have a party in Honeybrook.
The people come out of their houses again and cheer.
They're so happy!
Lilli is happy, too.
She parties with her friends into the morning.
Then her alarm goes off.

cheer – jubeln

Time to go back home to Leon and her mother. She wants to take her stuffed toy mouse out of her pocket – but it's not there.

WHERE CAN IT BE?

The witch's leap can't work without her stuffed toy mouse.

WHERE CAN IT BE?

And then Lilli knows . . . and panics. It's in Count Dracula's castle, in the cellar. She had it between her teeth and then she opened her mouth and screamed.

Darn! Darn! Darn! Not much time. She runs to the town square. The carriage. A girth. She presses the girth to her heart. The witch's leap!

girth – Sattelriemen

Back in the castle. She opens her rucksack.

The vampire's outfit. The cape. The vampire's teeth. No time for make-up.

Quick, Lilli, quick.

Through the door. Down the stairs.

Into the cellar. The coffins are empty.

There, Count Dracula’s coffin. And there’s the stuffed toy mouse. Lilli relaxes a little bit and picks it up.

“Hello!“

Oh no. Lilli knows who that is.

“Don’t turn around, Lilli,“ she says to herself. She hasn’t got

her sunglasses. "Don't look up, Lilli,"
she says to herself.
She knows that Count Dracula is standing behind her.
"I can smell human blood," Count Dracula says.
"Yes, it's here, come here, it's in the coffin," Lilli says.
She hears the Count. He's coming nearer. "Don't turn around now, Lilli," she says to herself again.

Count Dracula comes nearer
and looks into the coffin.
Now Lilli turns around quickly and runs.
Through the door, up the stairs.
She runs and runs.
Behind her she can hear Count Dracula. He runs and runs.
And then she can hear the other vampires behind him.
She presses the stuffed toy mouse to her heart, says the words for the witch's leap and keeps on running.

Nothing happens.
Maybe it's the stupid vampire's teeth. Maybe the words aren't clear enough.
Darn! Darn! Darn!

She spits out the teeth. She can still hear Count Dracula and the other vampires. She wants to say the words for the witch's leap again. And then she hears screams behind her.
Horrible screams.
The first flashes of sunlight! Don't turn around now. Are the vampires dead? Have they turned to dust?
"Don't turn around, Lilli," she says to herself again.

spits out – spuckt aus

Lilli presses the stuffed toy mouse to her heart . . .

“Lilli, how did you get here?“

Oh no, it’s Leon!

“Lilli, I don’t get it . . .“

And Lilli says: “Leon, you must knock on my door before you can come in.“

And then to herself:

“What a night . . .“

Liebe Eltern, liebe Lehrer,

Die meisten Kinder sind sehr stolz darauf, wenn sie ihr erstes Buch in einer fremden Sprache gelesen haben – zu Recht! Mit diesem einfachen und didaktisch aufgearbeiteten englischen *Hexe-Lilli*-Abenteuer können nun sogar schon Englisch-Anfänger begeistert und motiviert werden.
Der Text basiert auf einem Grundwortschatz von ca. 450 Wörtern, was ca. einem Dreivierteljahr Englischunterricht in der fünften Klasse einer weiterführenden Schule entspricht bzw. mit der flächendeckenden Einführung des Grundschulenglisch ca. einem halben Jahr.

Wir haben bei dieser englischen Fassung von *Hexe Lilli* die neuesten Erkenntnisse aus der Fremdsprachendidaktik zu Grunde gelegt.
Bisher ist man im (traditionellen) Fremdsprachenunterricht davon ausgegangen, dass Kinder einen Text in der Fremdsprache nur dann verstehen können, wenn ihnen sämtliche darin enthaltenen grammatischen Strukturen hinlänglich vertraut sind. Wenn Sie dieses Buch durchlesen, wird Ihnen auffallen, dass wir durchaus die Vergangenheit und die Zukunft benutzen oder auch vereinzelt Relativsätze. Dies sind Themen, die nach Lehrplan erst im Laufe der Klasse sechs unterrichtet werden.
Die neueren Forschungen über Ver-

stehensprozesse beim Lesen zeigen jedoch, dass ein Leser (unabhängig vom Alter) sich vor allem auf die inhaltlichen Informationen und nicht auf die grammatischen Informationen in einem Text konzentriert. Das heißt, in einem Satz wie “She will defend the town against the vampires.“ sind eigentlich nur drei Wörter interessant: defend – town – vampires, womit die entscheidenden Informationen genannt sind. Jeder Leser erschließt sich den Sinn ganz leicht selber. Das heißt für den Unterricht oder auch die Lektüre zu Hause, dass Kinder Texte lesen können, die sie inhaltlich verstehen – auch wenn sie die grammatischen Strukturen nicht kennen.
Auf diesen Erkenntnissen beruht der

vorliegende Text. Die Sätze haben wir möglichst kurz gehalten, die inhaltlich wichtigen Wörter sind den Kindern entweder bekannt, können aus dem Deutschen erschlossen werden oder werden erklärt. Auch die Illustrationen haben wir bewusst so ausgewählt, dass sie die Situation nochmals anschaulich darstellen.
Noch ein Wort zu den Vokabel-Erklärungen: Sie sollen Hürden abbauen und nicht neue Hürden schaffen. Deshalb haben wir sie – im Unterschied zu den gängigen Englisch-Lehrwerken – so verfasst, dass sie teilweise aus ganzen Phrasen bestehen und möglichst wenig grammatisches Wissen von den Lesern abverlangen (daher ist z.B. auf

die Infinitiv-Form mit “to“ verzichtet worden).

Damit Ihr Kind mit seinem ersten englischen *Hexe-Lilli*-Abenteuer zurechtkommt, gehen Sie doch bitte mit ihm gemeinsam die Lesetipps auf der letzten Seite durch. Jetzt kann eigentlich nichts mehr schief gehen!

Viel Spaß und viel Erfolg bei der Lektüre wünschen

Ellen Butzko und KNISTER

Hexe Lillis ganz geheime Lesetipps:

Wenn du nicht bei jedem Wort weißt, was es heißt, lies einfach weiter. Du wirst merken, die Geschichte verstehst du auch so!

Die Übersetzung von einigen schwierigeren Vokabeln findest du unten auf der jeweiligen Seite. Die übersetzten Vokabeln sind im Text unterstrichen.

Viele englische Wörter, die du noch nicht kennst, sind ganz ähnlich wie im Deutschen. Zum Beispiel: idea = Idee, brilliant = brilliant, press = pressen.

Manche Wörter wirst du wieder erkennen, weil sie im Deutschen auch verwendet werden. Zum Beispiel: skateboard, relax, rucksack.

Prima ist, dass du in diesem Buch auch Wörter lernst, die dir deine Englischlehrerin normalerweise nicht beibringt. Zum Beispiel: creep = blöder Kerl, darn = verflixt, nicht zu vergessen all die gefährlichen Vampir-Vokabeln wie suck blood = Blut saugen oder coffin = Sarg.

KNISTER

Hexe Lillis großes Geheimnis
Drei spannende Abenteuer für den Unterricht

Ob wilder Wilder Westen, Detektivabenteuer oder Fußballfieber – mit Hexe Lilli machen Lese- und Sprachübungen gleich dreimal so viel Spaß! Ergänzt werden Lillis spannende Geschichten mit didaktischem Material zu jedem Kapitel, konzipiert von der Grundschullehrerin Frauke Nahrgang. Da wird selbst der letzte Lesemuffel zur Leseratte!